ADA TWIST, SCIENTIST
THE WHY FILES

BUG BONANZA!

By Andrea Beaty and Dr. Theanne Griffith

Amulet Books • New York

To my grandmother, Lena Page —A.B.

To my partner in life and science, Jorge —T.G.

Library of Congress Control Number 2022944653

ISBN 978-1-4197-6555-1

ADA TWIST ™ Netflix. Used with permission.
Story and text © Andrea Beaty
ADA TWIST series imagery © Netflix, Inc. and used with permission from Netflix.
Ada Twist, Scientist and the Questioneers created by Andrea Beaty and David Roberts

Book design by Charice Silverman
Illustrations by Steph Stilwell

Printed and bound in U.S.A.

10 9 8 7 6 5 4 3 2 1

Amulet Books are available at special discounts when purchased in quantity for premiums and promotions as well as fundraising or educational use. Special editions can also be created to specification. For details, contact specialsales@abramsbooks.com or the address below.

Amulet Books® is a registered trademark of Harry N. Abrams, Inc.

Images courtesy Shutterstock.com: **Cover:** *bee,* Marco Tulio; *blue butterfly,* Vladimirkarp; *spider,* Subin Sailendran; *ladybug,* motorolka; *millipede,* asawinimages; *green bug,* irin-k; *magnifying glass,* Rtimages. **Pages i, 26, 27:** *blue butterflies,* Vladimirkarp. **Page 4:** *shrimp,* Mariusz W. **Page 5:** *crab,* Tatyana Domnicheva. **Pages 13, 27, 60, 61:** *bugs,* irin-k. **Page 17:** fotandy. **Page 19:** Komsan Loonprom. **Page 24:** *scientist with butterfly,* Elnur; *scientists looking at microscope,* Thammanoon Khamchalee. **Page 33:** Wirestock Creators. **Page 36:** *cobweb,* MelnikovSergei; *sheet web,* IanRedding. **Page 37:** Sari ONeal. **Page 39:** *sheet web in grass,* Bildagentur Zoonar GmbH. **Page 41:** xtotha. **Page 42:** kooanan007. **Page 44:** Alex Stemmers. **Page 45:** zatvornik. **Page 46:** Jr images. **Page 50:** OSDG. **Page 51:** Jarous. **Page 53:** *shrimp,* David Tadevosian. **Page 55:** *millipede,* somyot pattana. **Pages 57, 64:** Marco Tulio **Page 59:** Fercast. **Page 61:** D Busquets. *School supplies throughout,* Green Leaf. ***Images courtesy public domain:*** **Cover:** *orange butterfly,* ksblack99; *flower,* Marianne Cornelissen-Kuyt. **Page 3:** *ants,* kazuend; *spider,* ViajeroExtraviado; *centipede,* AchimRodekohr. **Page 4:** *spider,* Leon Brooks. **Page 6:** Jessica Towne. **Page 12:** jms85. **Page 16:** Kaldari. **Page 20:** *cockroach,* Brett_Hondow. **Page 27:** *illustration,* Maria Sibylla Merian. **Page 29:** Katja Schulz. **Page 35:** *spiral orb web,* Johann Ravera; *funnel web,* GerritR. **Page 38:** pasja1000. **Page 39:** *indoor cobweb,* GerDukes. **Page 40:** Josefka. **Page 43:** imakeitsolutions. **Page 53:** *crab,* Dav Pape. **Page 55:** *bee,* Alabama Extension. **Page 58:** Charles J. Sharp. **Page 62:** K Bahr. **Page 67:** *grass,* Josh Pollock; *insect,* USFWS Midwest Region.

ABRAMS The Art of Books
195 Broadway, New York, NY 10007
abramsbooks.com

I was in the garden when a bug jumped onto a flower! I looked closer. There were bugs on the leaves. Bugs on the ground. There were even bugs in the air!

Some were creepy and crawly.
Some were wiggly and jiggly.
Some were very buzzy.
They were everywhere!
And they were all different.

Fascinating!

WHAT ARE BUGS?

It's a mystery! A riddle! A puzzle! A quest!

Time to find out what bugs are about!

We call ants, spiders, and centipedes bugs. They are very different, but they are all related. Scientists call these animals **arthropods**.

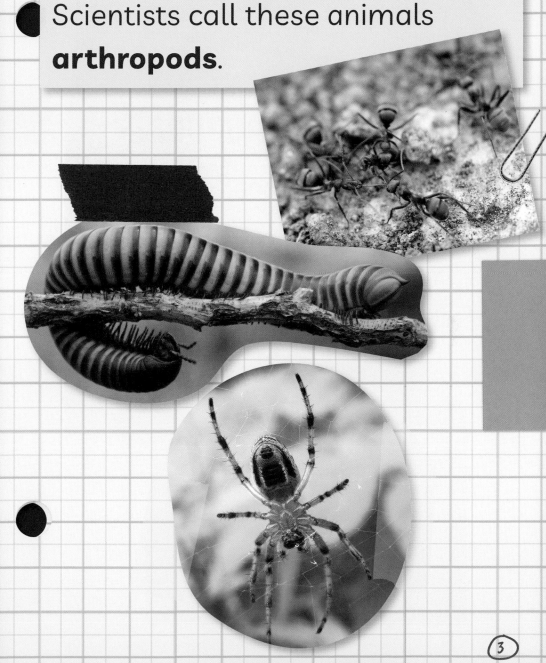

AMAZING ARTHROPODS

- There are 1,170,000 kinds of arthropods.

- Arthropods make up 80% of all animals!

- Insects, spiders, millipedes, and even crabs and shrimp are all arthropods.

- Arthropods have no bones!

- They also don't have skin!

Bug bodies are very different than human bodies. Humans have bones inside our bodies that support us. Bugs don't! They have a hard covering called an **exoskeleton** that protects them. For example, the shell around a beetle is an exoskeleton.

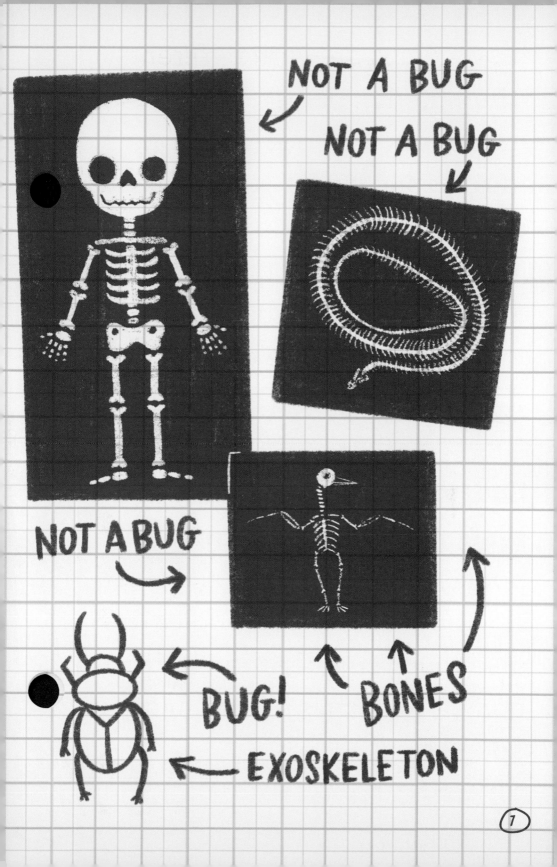

Bug bodies are made up of sections called **segments**. Our bodies are not as neatly divided as a bug's body. Bug bodies are also much smaller than human bodies—which is probably a good thing!

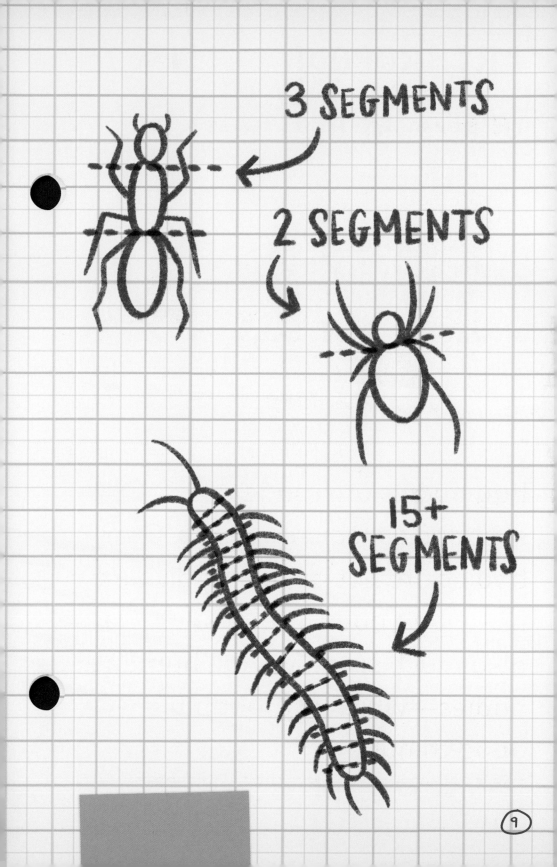

3 SEGMENTS

2 SEGMENTS

15+ SEGMENTS

⑨

ARTHROPOD!

(A poem by Ada Twist)

I lifted up a log

and what did I see?

A whole lot of bugs

looking up at me.

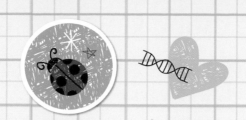

Some were wiggly and jiggly
and some were quite odd.
But every single one of them
was an arthropod!

There are many kinds of bugs. Let's learn more about them!

Insects are the most diverse group of arthropods. There are anywhere from six to ten million different species of insects on our planet!

HOW MANY BODY SEGMENTS DOES AN INSECT HAVE?

Insect bodies are divided into three segments: **head**, **thorax** (THOR-ax), and **abdomen** (AB-doh-men—it's a fancy way to say *belly*!).

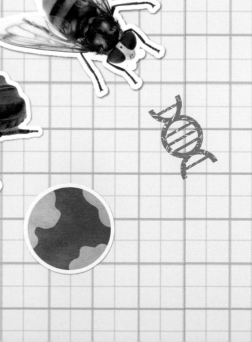

The PARTS of an INSECT

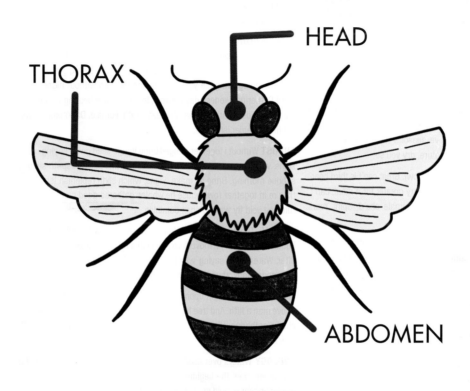

HEAD

THORAX

ABDOMEN

The head of an insect holds its antennas, mouth, and eyes. Adult insects can have two types of eyes.

Simple eyes can see only movement and light. They cannot see shapes and sizes.

Simple eyes

For example, an insect that has simple eyes cannot see the difference between a rose and a tulip, or a house and a car.

The other kind of eye found in insects is called a **compound eye**.

Compound eyes can see shapes and sizes. They are made of hundreds of little eyes. Each little eye sends a picture to the insect brain. The insect brain takes those small pictures and turns them into a big one.

Compound eyes

18

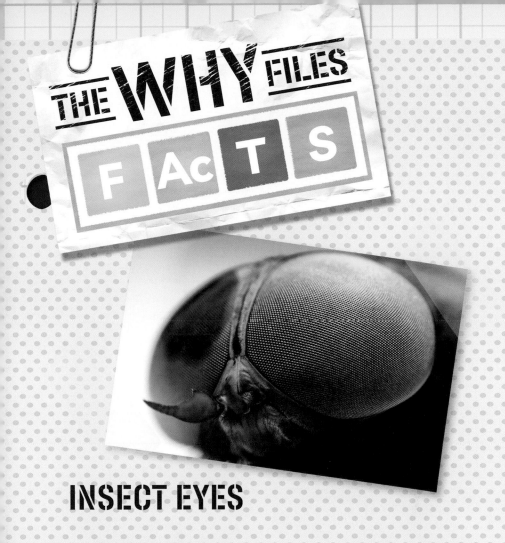

INSECT EYES

- Some insects have only simple eyes.

- Some insects have both simple and compound eyes.

- There are no insects that have only compound eyes. They must have simple eyes, too!

- Most insects have one to three simple eyes.

- The fly compound eye is made of about 800 little eyes!

- The cockroach compound eye is made of about 2,000 little eyes!

The middle part of an insect is called its **thorax**. Insects have six legs that stick out of the thorax. There are three legs on each side.

Some insects also have one or two pairs of wings. Insects have very strong muscles in their thorax. These strong muscles help them move all those legs and wings!

Insects also use their thorax to breathe. But they do not use lungs to breathe like we do. They use little holes in their thorax.

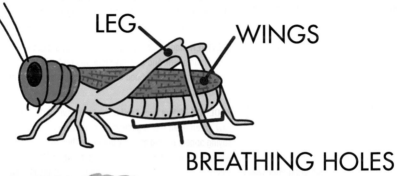

HOW INSECTS BREATHE

LEG

WINGS

BREATHING HOLES

The last segment of an insect is called the **abdomen**. This is the insect's belly. Just like our bellies, the abdomens of insects digest food and push out waste. The abdomen also holds the insect's heart.

There are so many insects and so much to know about them.

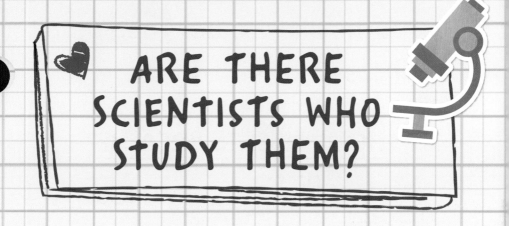

ARE THERE SCIENTISTS WHO STUDY THEM?

Yes, there are!

Entomology (en-toh-MOL-uh-jee) is the science of insects. Scientists have been curious about insects for thousands of years. By studying them, scientists have learned about the many important roles insects play in our environment.

ARISTOTLE (384–322 BC), a Greek scientist, was the first person to describe the different parts of insects in fourth century BC—more than 2,000 years ago!

MARIA SIBYLLA MERIAN (1647–1717) was the first woman insect scientist in Europe. She was also an artist. She made beautiful drawings of nearly 200 different kinds of insects.

CHARLES H. TURNER (1867–1923) was the first Black American insect scientist. He studied how ants and bees behave. He also discovered that bees could see both colors and patterns.

MARGARET S. COLLINS (1922–1996) was the first Black American woman insect scientist. She studied how termites survive in very hot and dry environments.

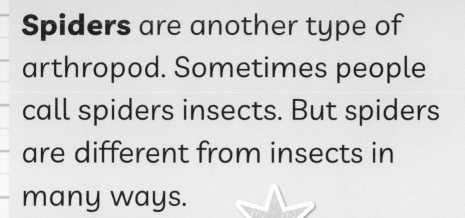

Spiders are another type of arthropod. Sometimes people call spiders insects. But spiders are different from insects in many ways.

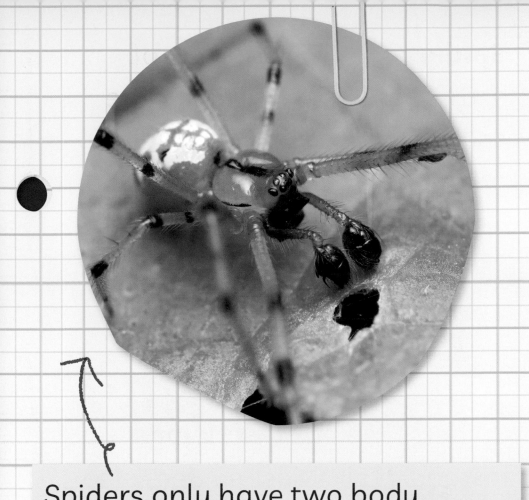

Spiders only have two body segments. Their head and thorax are joined together to make one segment. This segment is called the **prosoma** (pro-SO-ma). It is where the eyes, mouth, and legs of spiders are found.

Spiders also have eight legs instead of six. Most spiders also have eight simple eyes! Spiders do not have antennas.

Does it have antennas?

NO

YES

TRAIT	SPIDERS	INSECTS
Body segments	2	3
Number of legs	6	8
Eyes	Simple only	Always has simple eyes, might have complex eyes, too!
Antennas	Nope!	Yup!

NO

YES

YES

The abdomen of a spider holds its stomach, heart, and an organ that makes silk for webs.

On the spider's abdomen there are two slits. Kind of like gills on a fish! Inside these slits are special spider lungs called **book lungs**. Book lungs get their name because they are made of thin "pages" or pockets that fill with air.

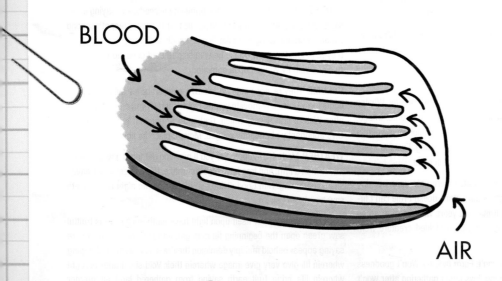

BLOOD

AIR

I found a spiderweb stretched between two branches of a tree. It was beautiful.

WHY DO SPIDERS MAKE WEBS? DO ALL SPIDERS MAKE WEBS?

Spiders are hunters. They mostly eat insects. Many spiders build webs out of silk and use them to catch prey. But not all webs are the same!

WONDERFUL WEBS

- **SPIRAL ORB WEBS** are large webs that have the shape of a circle. They look like wheels!

- **FUNNEL WEBS** are flat and have a tube that leads to the spider's nest.

- **COBWEBS** are sticky and messy. They don't have a regular shape and are also called tangle webs.

- **SHEET WEBS** are flat like a mat and thick with many layers.

The type of web a spider spins tells you what kind of spider it is. For example, black widow spiders make funnel webs.

A REAL black widow spider!

The type of web also tells you where they live. Most spiders that spin spiral orb webs are near forests or gardens. You can find funnel webs in between rocks and plants. Many corners will have a cobweb or two. And sheet webs stretch across grass or branches.

Not all spiders spin webs. Tarantulas are hairy spiders that don't make webs. They jump on their prey to catch them! Wolf spiders also jump to catch their prey.

Both tarantulas and wolf spiders build **burrows**. A burrow is a small hole or tunnel that is used as a home.

I picked up a rock in the garden and there was a worm. Except it wasn't a worm. It had legs! Lots and lots of legs! What was it?

Millipedes and **centipedes** are another group of arthropod. These critters have many segments, not just two or three!

Most millipedes are born
with six segments. Millipedes
can grow up to one foot long
and have up to one hundred
segments! Centipedes can have
up to 177 segments. But most
only have fifteen.

Both millipedes and centipedes are found all over the world. They like to live in wet and damp places. But they can also live in the desert! They have even been found in the Arctic Circle—the North Pole!

Millipedes and centipedes also have differences. Centipedes eat insects, spiders, and even other centipedes. Millipedes don't eat other bugs. They eat rotten wood, plants, or leaves.

Millipedes also have more legs than centipedes. Millipedes have two pairs of legs that stick out of each body segment. Centipedes only have one pair of legs in each segment.

MILLIPEDE

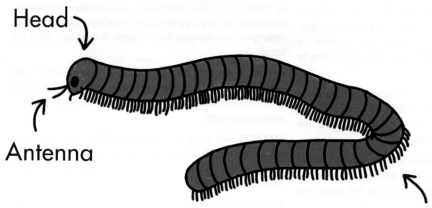

Head

Antenna

2 Pairs of Legs Per
Body Segment

CENTIPEDE

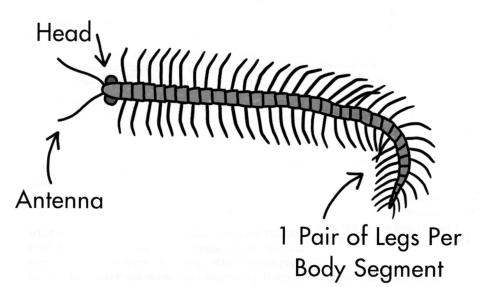

Head

Antenna

1 Pair of Legs Per
Body Segment

TRAIT	MILLIPEDES	CENTIPEDES
Number of segments	Up to 100!	Up to 177!
Legs per segment	2	1
Favorite food	Wood, plants, leaves	Insects, spiders, other centipedes
Where they live	Just about everywhere!	Just about everywhere!

Insects, spiders, millipedes, and centipedes are all arthropods. And so are crabs, lobsters, and shrimp!

We don't think of these animals as bugs, but they are a part of the arthropod family.

horseshoe crab!

For example, a crab's protective shell is its exoskeleton. And horseshoe crabs don't have bones! And similar to the book lungs that spiders use to breathe, horseshoe crabs use **book gills**. In fact, horseshoe crabs are more closely related to spiders than they are to other crabs!

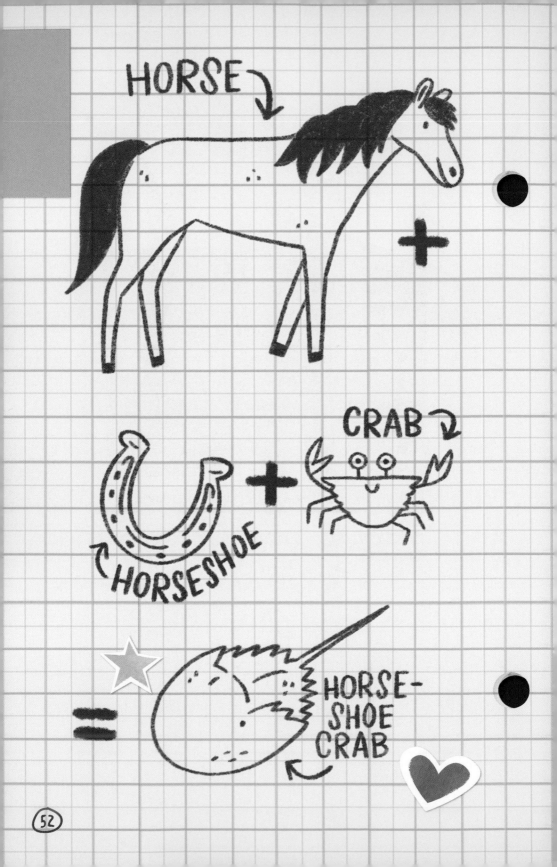

HORSE

+

HORSESHOE + CRAB

= HORSE-SHOE CRAB

Some people are scared of bugs. But most are harmless!

There are about 40,000 kinds of spiders in the United States. But only four of them are dangerous.

Millipedes may have lots of creepy legs, but they are very shy. They might even curl up into a ball if you surprise them!

Bees are insects that can sting, but they sting humans only when they are scared.

Bugs are cool! There are lots more of them than there are people. But that's good. We need bugs!

Bugs are very important members of our environment. Bugs such as bees help us grow fruit by spreading pollen from flower to flower.

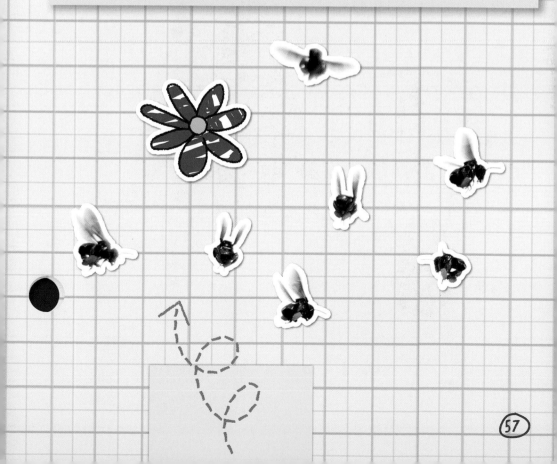

dung beetle

dung = poop!

Bugs that live in soil help keep it healthy so that we can grow yummy foods. Many bugs that live on land help keep our planet clean by breaking down waste such as dead plants and animals. Some bugs even eat poop!

Bugs are also food for many animals. Some frogs eat flies, some birds eat beetles, and even bats eat bugs! Bugs that live in water are also food for animals like fish.

And what about people?

CAN PEOPLE EAT BUGS, TOO?

YES!

THE WHY FILES

F Ac T S

- About two billion people from many cultures around the world eat insects as part of their normal diet.

- Cicadas are a popular insect treat in some parts of the United States! They have lots of protein, which makes you strong.

- In the south of Brazil, giant winged ants are also eaten. The wings are taken off and the ants are then fried and dipped in chocolate. Yummy!

- Crabs, lobsters, and shrimp are arthropods, so if you've eaten those before, you've eaten a bug, too!

- Eating bugs is good for Earth. Growing bugs doesn't produce as many greenhouse gases as raising farm animals used for food, like cows or pigs. Greenhouse gases make our planet too warm.

Bugs are important members of our planet. But the number of bugs is dropping around the world. Humans are taking up more space, which means bugs have fewer places to make homes. And as Earth gets warmer, it is becoming harder for bugs to find food.

If there are fewer bugs, there will also be less food for animals like birds, reptiles, and fish.

We really need bugs! Losing bugs is a big problem. Maybe we can help in lots of little but mighty ways! But how?

We could help bugs by planting different kinds of wildflowers in a garden. That would give bees lots of choices for food. The more types of flowers that bees can visit, the happier they are! And when bees are happy, they make more honey. And more bees!

Happy bees also spread more pollen. That helps us grow A LOT of the food we eat, like fruits and vegetables. We need bees! Without them, we would have a lot less food to eat.

We can also build bug hotels! They are just like birdhouses. They give bugs protection and shelter.

Letting grass grow tall is another good way to help bugs. Tall grass and leaves help bugs hide. We can help bugs by leaving grass in one part of the yard or garden to grow long.

We can make a difference!

I have MORE QUESTIONS now than I did before.

Why does each question lead to three questions more?

Is answering that what science is for?

MY QUESTIONS!

How do spiders communicate with each other?

My brother calls me "crabby" when I am cranky. Do crabs get crabby?

What is the biggest insect in the world?

Why do ants follow each other in a line?

How do bees find flowers?

Can moths see in the dark?

Are there insects at the North Pole or South Pole?

What is the tiniest arthropod in the world?

Can butterflies swim?

Can beetles play guitars?

Are the Beatles arthropods?

SIMPLE
SCIENCE
EXPERIMENTS

You can ask a grown-up for help!

BUILD A BUG HOTEL!

MATERIALS

An old wooden box or crate*

Any combination of the materials below will work. Be creative!

- twigs
- leaves
- scrap cardboard
- toilet paper rolls
- wood chips
- rolled-up paper
- pieces of bark
- hollowed-out branches or small logs

*You can also use an old plant pot tipped on its side, a recycled wooden drawer, or an old birdhouse with the front removed.

INSTRUCTIONS

1 Decide what structure you will use for your bug hotel.

2 Gather the materials you will place inside your hotel. It can be any combination of what is listed above.

3 Place materials inside of your bug hotel. Bugs like to hide! Toilet paper rolls make good bug hideouts.

4 Fill the hotel with materials, but also leave room for the bugs to create their homes. You may have to move materials around as you fill it up.

5 Place your bug hotel in a darker place with some shelter. It could be next to the garden or a woodpile, or near shrubs and bushes.

6 Observe! What kinds of critters visit your bug hotel? You can also make two or more hotels with different materials inside and compare visitors. This will help you learn about which environments different bugs prefer!

Share your bug hotels on social media using #whyfileswonders!

LET'S TRY ANOTHER EXPERIMENT!

WEAVE AN ORB WEB!

MATERIALS

- Popsicle sticks

- Glue or a hot glue gun*

- Yarn

- Scissors

- Paint (optional)

*If using a hot glue gun, parental supervision is advised.

INSTRUCTIONS

1. Glue three Popsicle sticks together. It should look like a snowflake pattern. Let the glue dry completely.

2 Once dry, you can paint the Popsicle sticks (optional). If painted, wait until paint is dry.

3 Cut a piece of yarn that is about 3 to 4 feet long.

4 Tie the end of the yarn into a knot in the middle of your Popsicle web.

5 Wrap the yarn over one Popsicle stick, and then under the next Popsicle stick. Repeat over, under, over, under to build your web!

6 When you are done wrapping the yarn, tie the end to the last Popsicle stick.

Share your webs on social media using #whyfileswonders!

Andrea Beaty

is the bestselling author of the Questioneers series and many other books. She has a degree in biology and computer science. Andrea lives outside Chicago where she writes books for kids and plants flowers for birds, bees, and bugs. Learn more about her books at AndreaBeaty.com.

Sirk Productions

Theanne Griffith, PhD,

is a brain scientist by day and a storyteller by night. She is the lead investigator of a neuroscience laboratory at the University of California–Davis and author of the science adventure series The Magnificent Makers. She lives in Northern California with her family. Learn more about her STEM-themed books at TheanneGriffith.com.

Samantha Jovan Photography

CHECK OUT THESE OTHER BOOKS STARRING
ADA TWIST, SCIENTIST

There's more to discover at **Questioneers.com.**

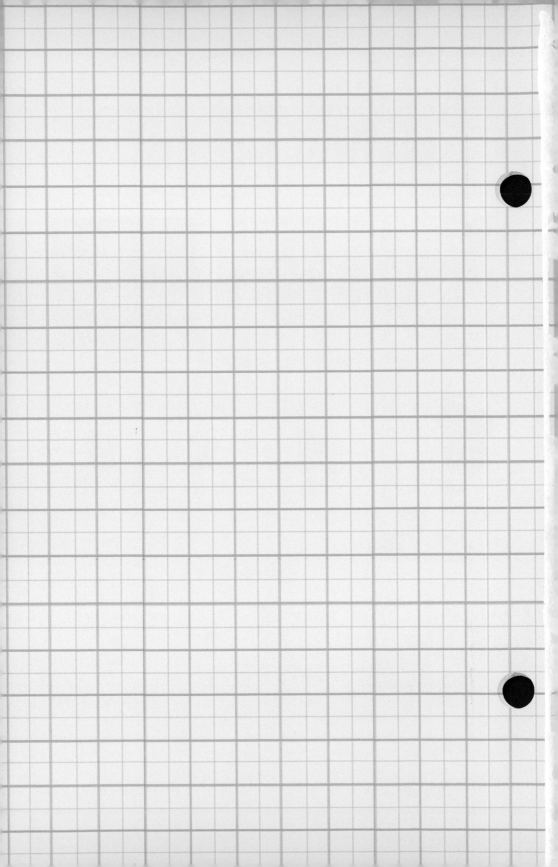